HOW TO DRAW IN
4 STYLES

Contents

Introduction   4

Introduction

Welcome to "How to Draw in 4 Levels"!

Within this book, you'll discover a simple and enjoyable experience with easy-to-follow step-by-step illustrations. This guide is packed with drawing ideas that will take you through four levels, from simple sketches to creations full of surprises.

The steps will be shown from left to right and top to bottom. Follow along and watch your artwork come to life with each progressive step.

What will you need to start drawing:

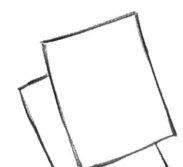

Papers: serves as a fundamental medium for sketching, painting.

Pencils: can be used for sketching, shading, and creating detailed drawings.

Erasers: can be used for correcting errors, lightening or erasing lines, and creating highlights in their drawings

Pencil sharpener: can be used for maintaining the sharpness of their drawing pencils.

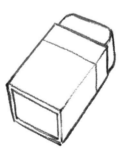

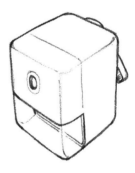

Alright, grab your tools and get drawing!

Plastic bottle

Basic

Simple

Better

Mike Dios

Artist

Plastic bottle

Basic	Simple	Better	Artist

Cell phone

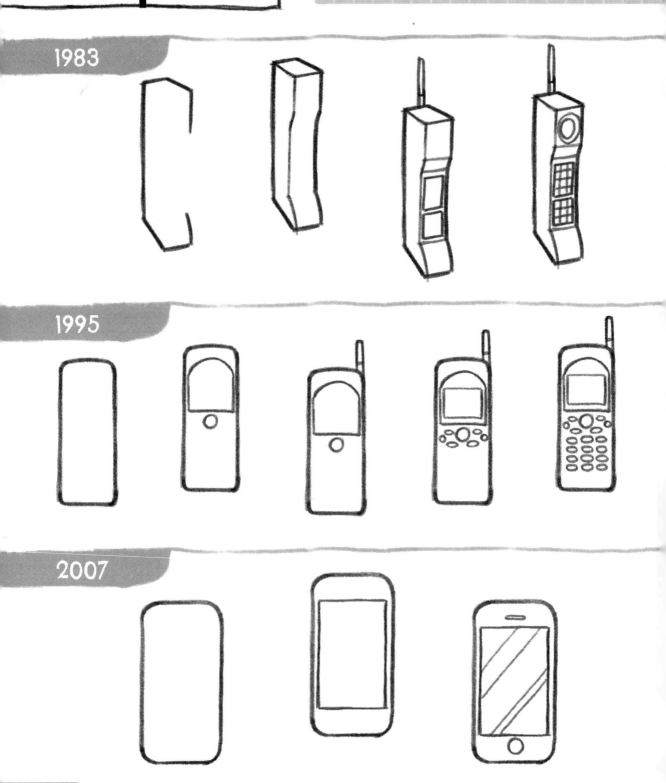

1983

1995

2007

Mike Dios

2023

Cell phone

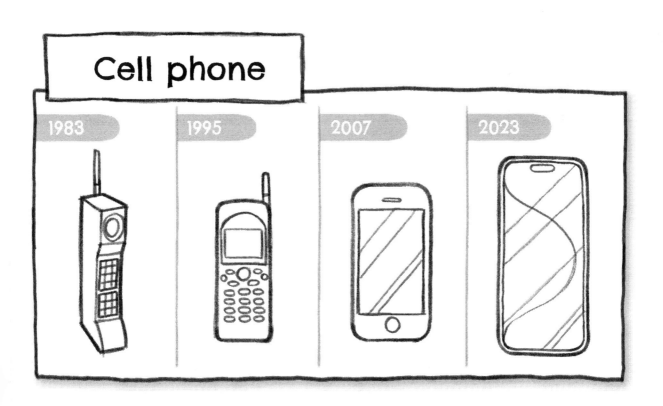

Bird

Experienced

Legend

Who drew like this when you were a kid?

Bird

Noob

Novice

Experienced

Legend

Mike Dios

Money

Basic

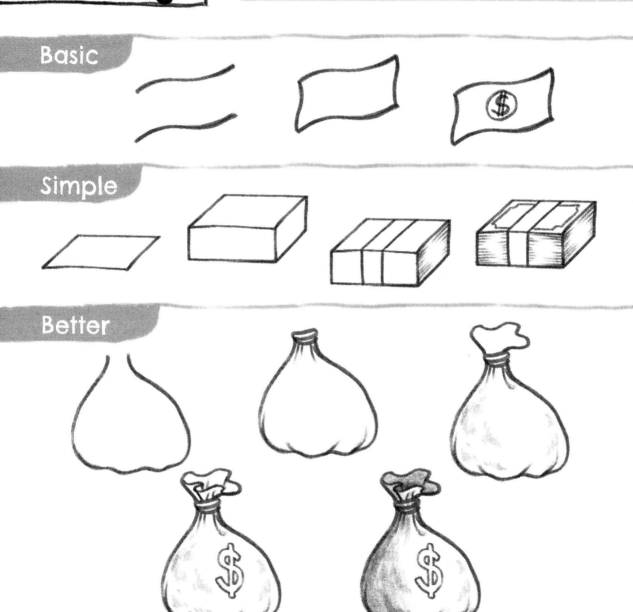

Simple

Better

Realistic

Mastercard

Money

Basic

Simple

Better

Realistic

Mastercard

Watch

Beginner

Learning

Pro

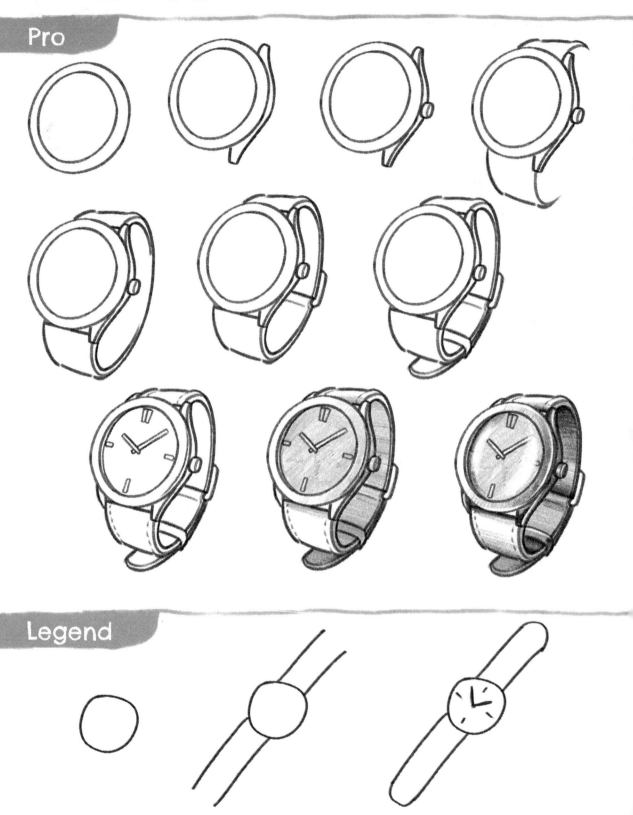

Legend

Mike Dios

Watch

Beginner

Learning

Pro

Legend

Coffee

Raw

Simple

Better

Mike Dios

Realistic

OOPS!

Coffee

Raw

Simple

Better

Realistic

Microphone

Basic

Simple

Better

Pro

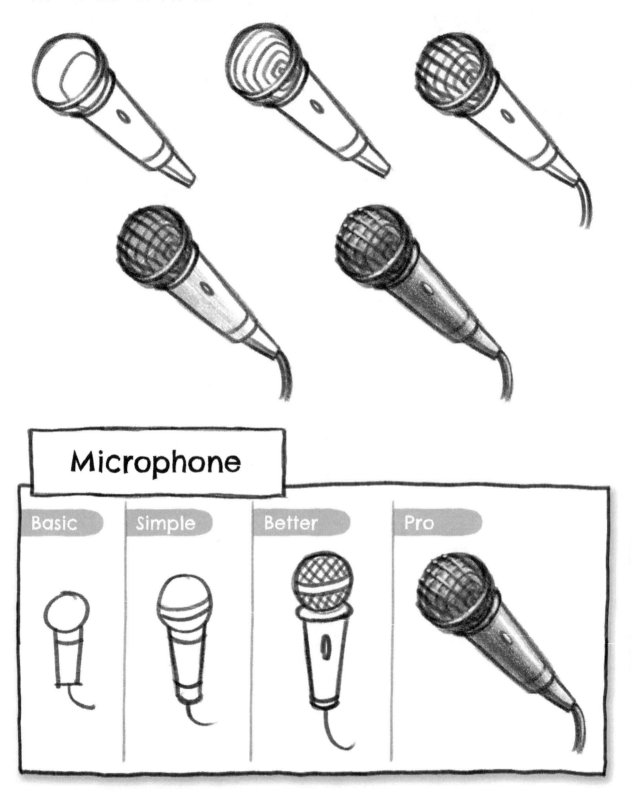

Microphone

Basic

Simple

Better

Pro

Mike Dios

Letter "A"

Basic

Simple

Better

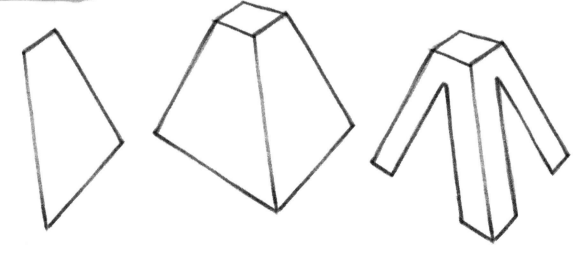

Mike Dios 23

Impossible

Letter "A"

Basic

Simple

Better

Impossible

Heart

Broken

3D

On fire

Legend

Heart

Broken

3D

On fire

Heart on fire

Legend

Ant

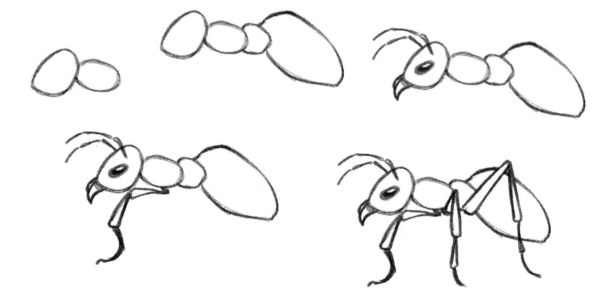

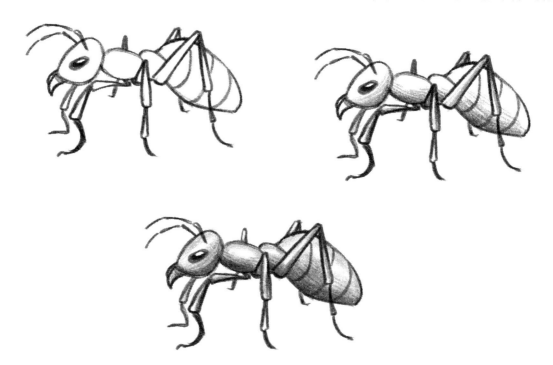

Realistic

You might need a magnifier glass with this.

Ant

Noob

Learning

Experienced

Realistic

Ball

Basic

American

Better

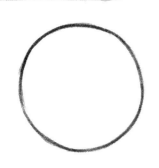 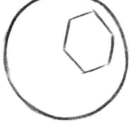  

Artist

Ball

Basic

American

Better

Artist

Cow

Pro

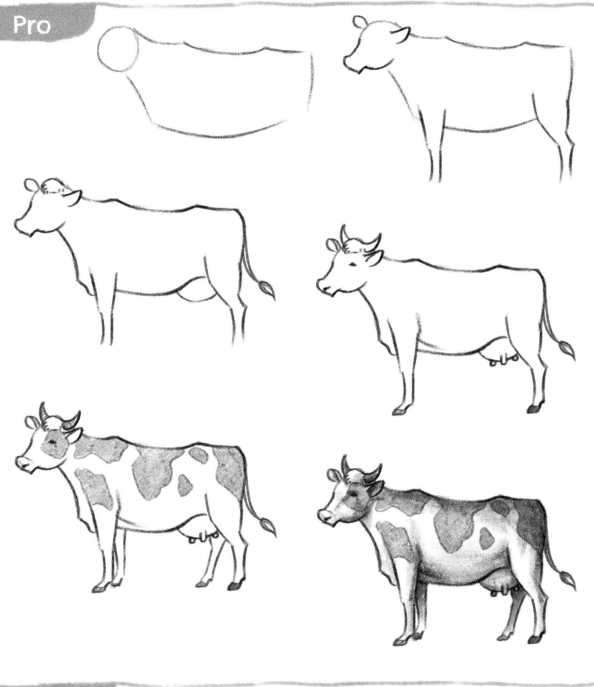

Chef

Cow

Child

Learning

Pro

Chef

Ice-cream

Basic

Simple

Cute

Realistic

Ice-cream

Basic

Realistic

Cat

Basic

Simple

Better

How to draw in 4 levels

Perfect

Cat

Basic

Simple

Better

Perfect

Star

Basic

Simple

Advance

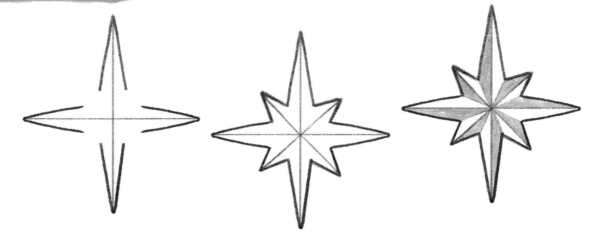

Impossible

Mike Dios 43

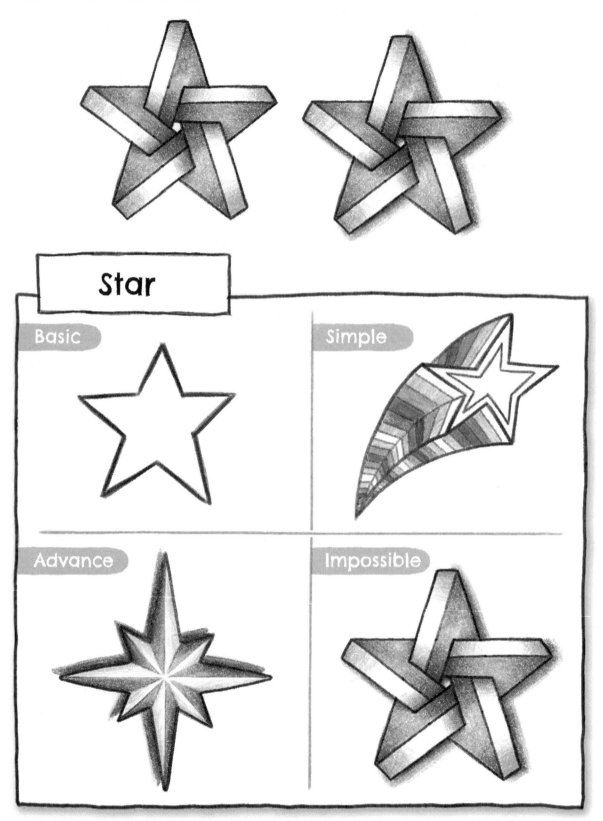

Star

Basic

Simple

Advance

Impossible

Flower

Basic

Simple

Better

Artist

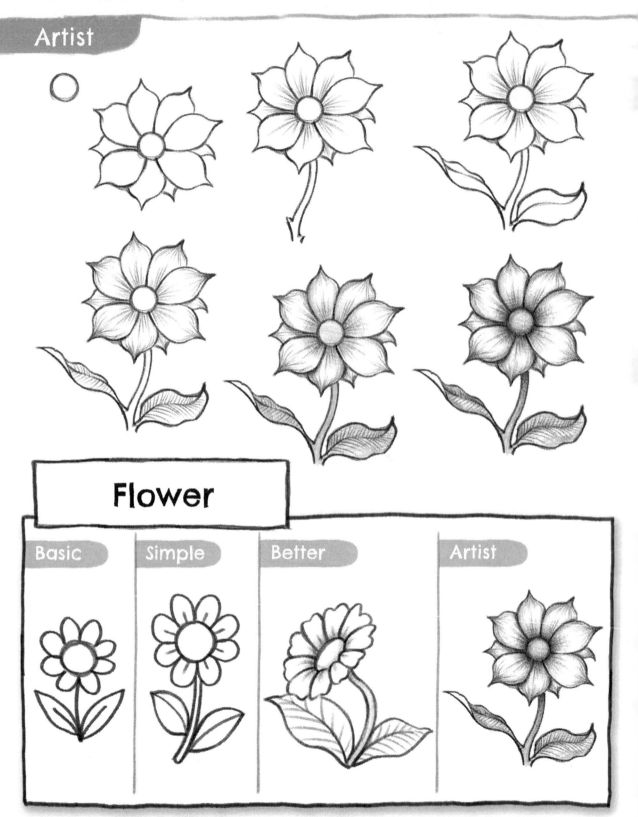

Flower

Basic	Simple	Better	Artist

Dog

Basic

Simple

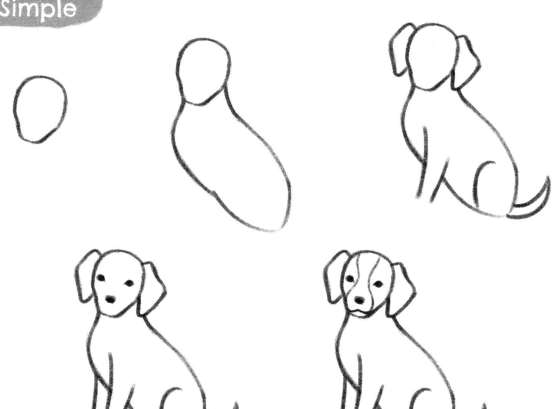

Better

Perfect

Dog

Basic

Simple

Better

Perfect

Bubble tea

Basic

Simple

Better

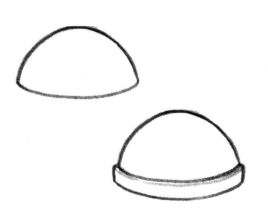  

Mike Dios

Kawaii

Bubble tea

Basic

Simple

Better

Kawaii

Fish

Child

Learning

Artist

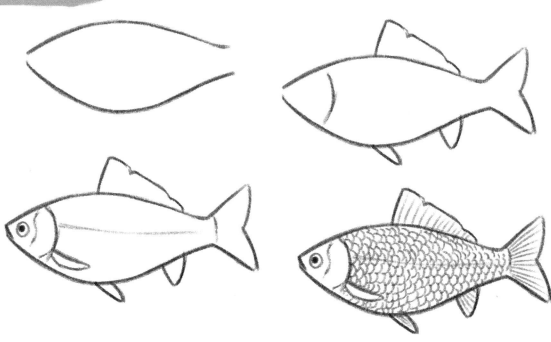

Japanese

Fish

Child

Learning

Artist

Japanese

Manta ray

Basic

Simple

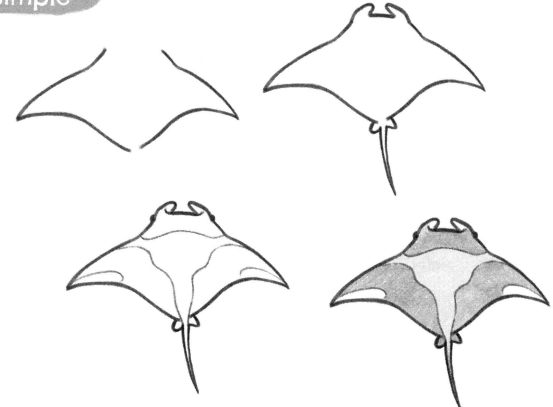

Better

Mike Dios

Artist

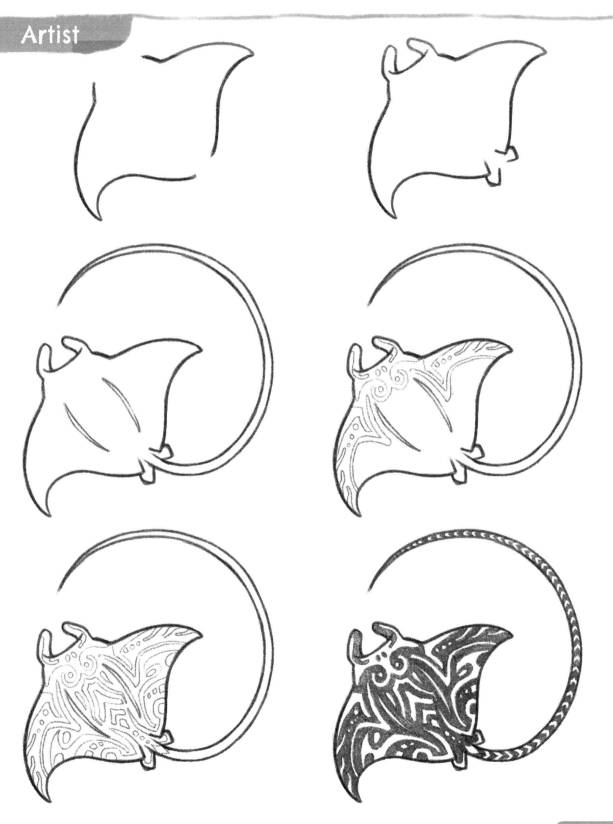

Manta ray

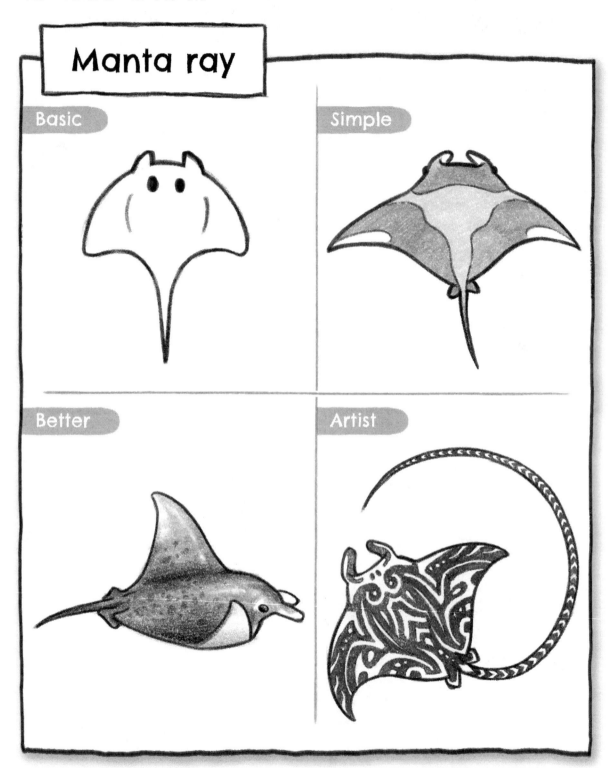

Basic

Simple

Better

Artist

Sneaker

Learning

Experienced

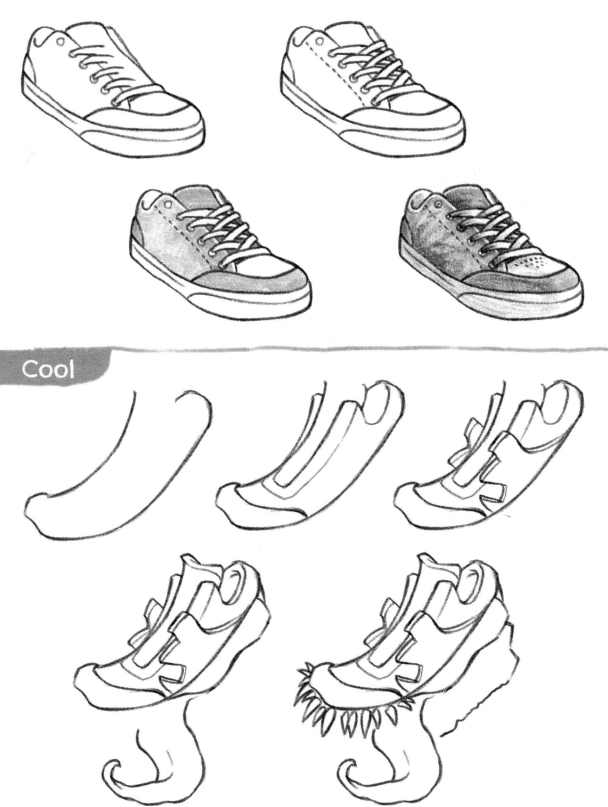

Cool

Mike Dios

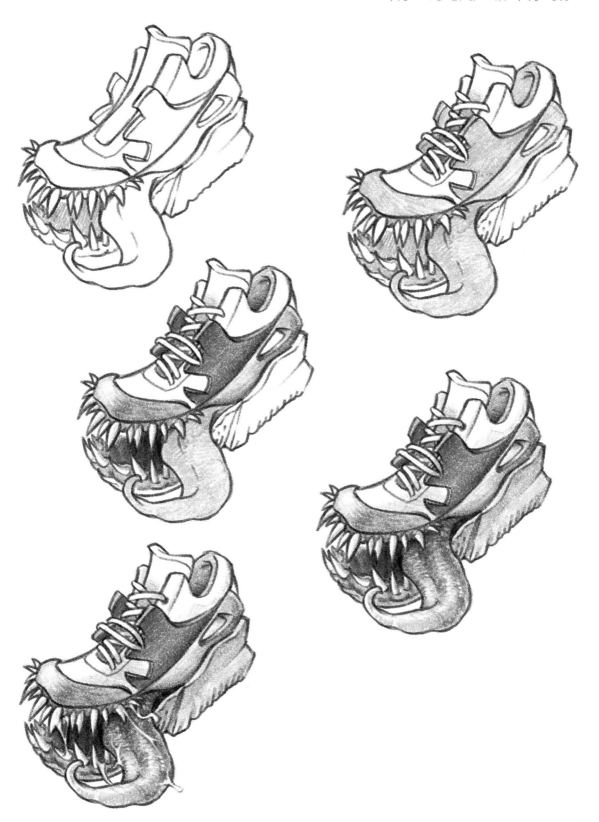

Sneaker

Noob

Beginner

Experienced

Artist

Mike Dios

Ghost

Basic

Simple

Better

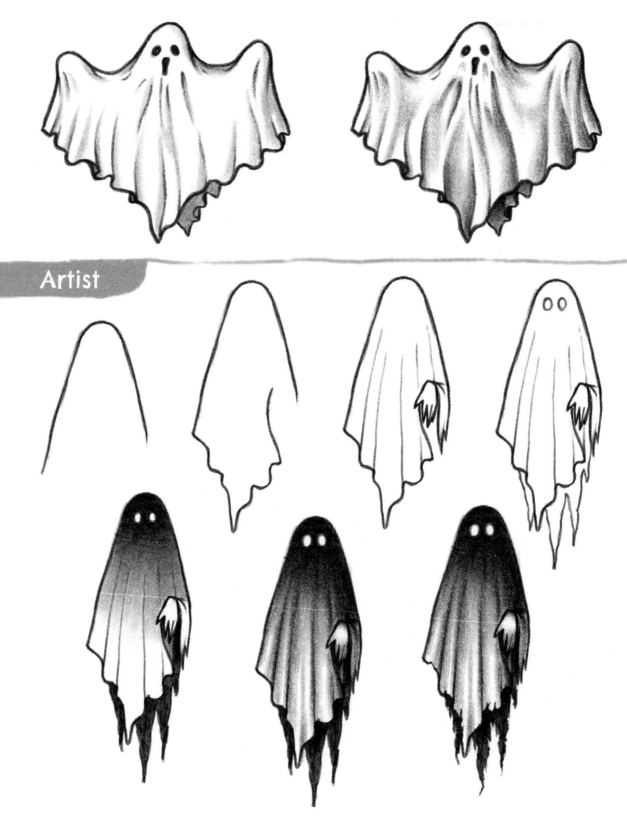

Artist

Mike Dios

Ghost

Basic

Simple

Better

Artist

Hat

Basic

Cowboy

Firefighter

Witch

Hat

Basic

Cowboy

Firefighter

Witch

Mike Dios

Frog

Simple

Learning

Pro

How to draw in 4 levels

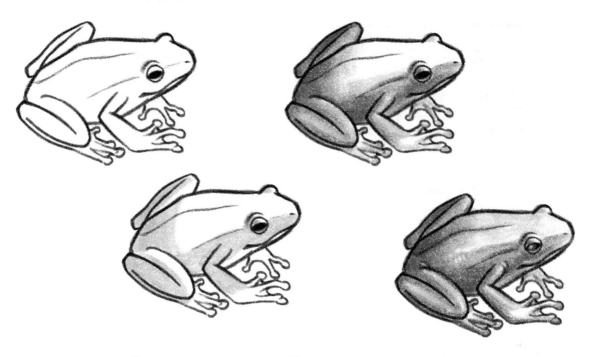

Perfect

Mike Dios

Frog

Simple

Learning

Pro

Perfect

Skull

Basic

Simple

Better

  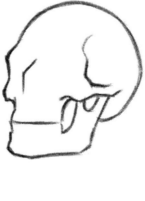 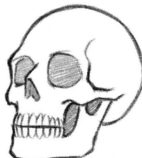

Mike Dios

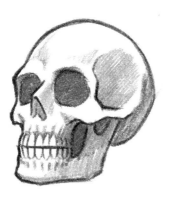

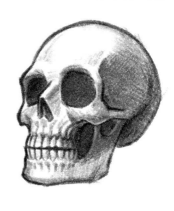

Artist

Mike Dios

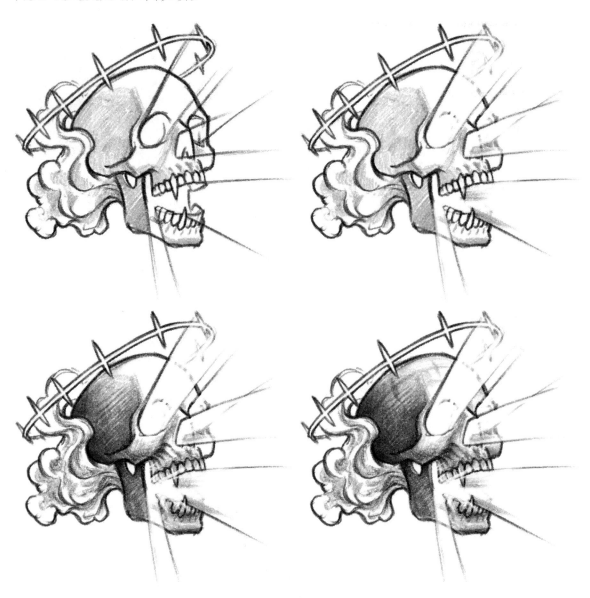

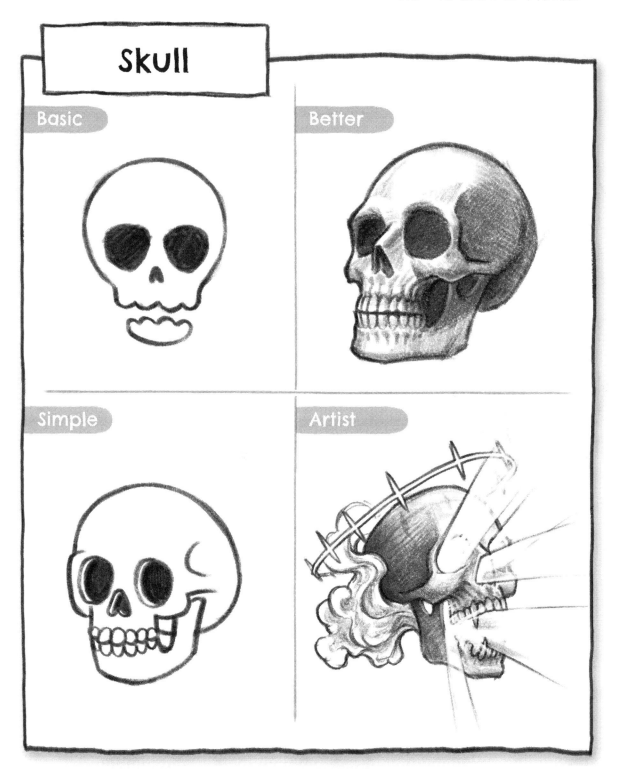

Skull

Basic

Better

Simple

Artist

Eye

Basic

Simple

Better

Mike Dios

Artist

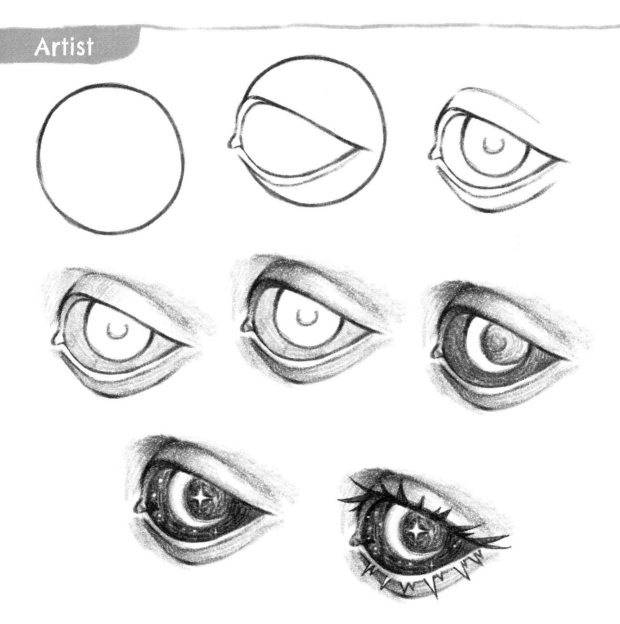

Eye

Basic

Simple

Better

Artist

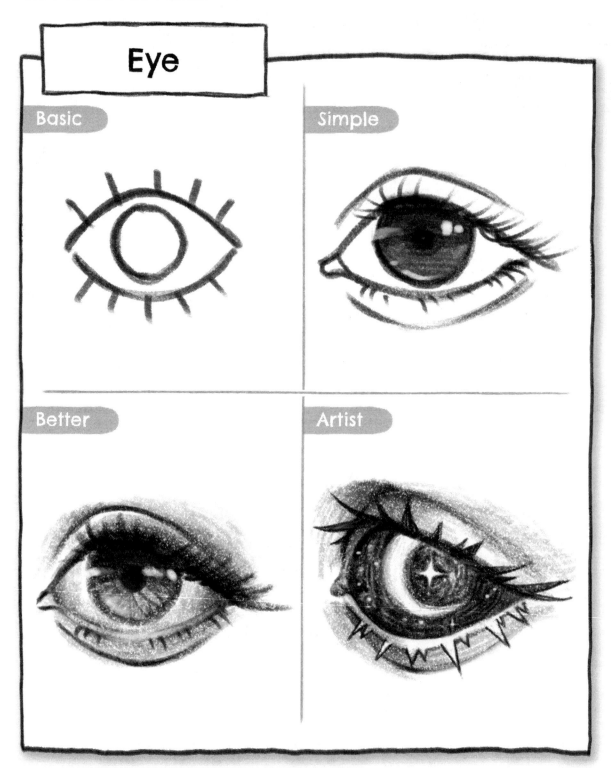

Lizard

Basic

Simple

Better

How to draw in 4 levels

Mike Dios

Lizard

Basic

Simple

Better

Artist

Mushroom

Noob

Beginner

Pro

Artist

Mike Dios

Mushroom

Noob

Beginner

Pro

Artist

Face

Basic

Simple

Anime

Mike Dios

Realistic

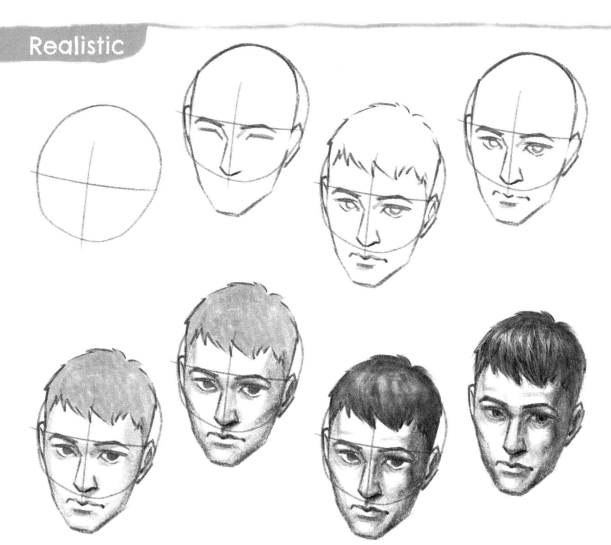

Face

Basic

Simple

Anime

Realistic

Mike Dios

Seahorse

Basic

Simple

Better

How to draw in 4 levels

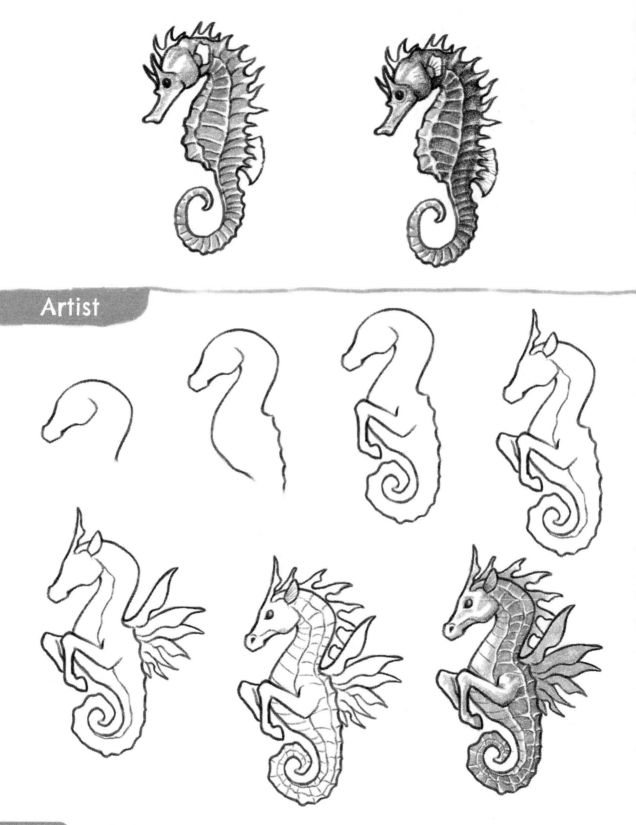

Artist

Seahorse

Basic **Simple** **Better** **Artist**

Made in United States
Troutdale, OR
12/09/2024

25705370R00053